JOURNEY
GREATEST HITS

T0047554

Contents

UPDATED EDITION

Produced by
Alfred Music Publishing Co., Inc.
P.O. Box 10003
Van Nuys, CA 91410-0003
alfred.com

Printed in USA.

ISBN-10: 0-7390-6878-4
ISBN-13: 978-0-7390-6878-6

ONLY THE YOUNG

Words and Music by
NEAL SCHON, JONATHAN CAIN
and STEVE PERRY

Moderately fast ♩ = 148

Verse 1:

1. An - oth - er night in an - y town. You can hear the

thun - der of their cry.

A - head of____ their time,

they won - der

why.__

Verses 2–4:

2. In the shad - ows of a gold - en age,___ a gen - er -
3. They're see - in' through the prom - is - es___ and all the
4. *Guitar solo ad lib.*

a - tion waits for dawn. Is it
lies they dare to tell.

Brave car - ry on; They
heav - en___ or hell?

bold and___ the strong.___ }
know ver - y well.___ }

young can say.

On - ly the young can say. On - ly the

young can say.

Repeat ad lib. and fade

DON'T STOP BELIEVIN'

Words and Music by
JONATHAN CAIN, NEAL SCHON
and STEVE PERRY

Moderate rock ♩ = 120

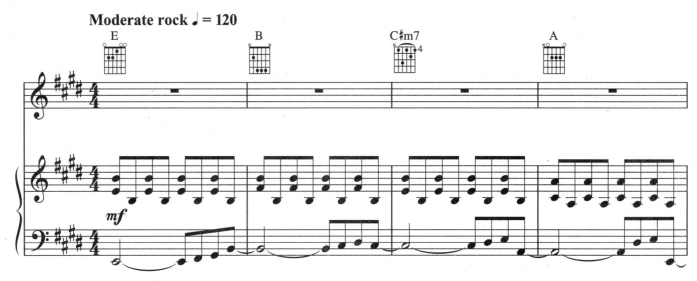

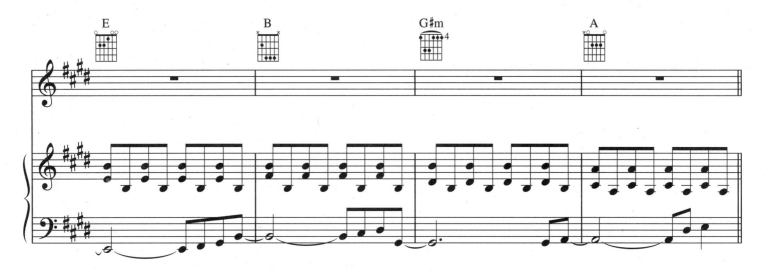

1. Just a small-town girl,___ livin' in a born and raised in
2. Just a city boy,___ the smell of wine and
3. A sing-er in a smok-y room,___ Ev-'ry-bod-y
4. Work-ing hard to get my fill.___ some were born to
5. Some will win and some will lose,___

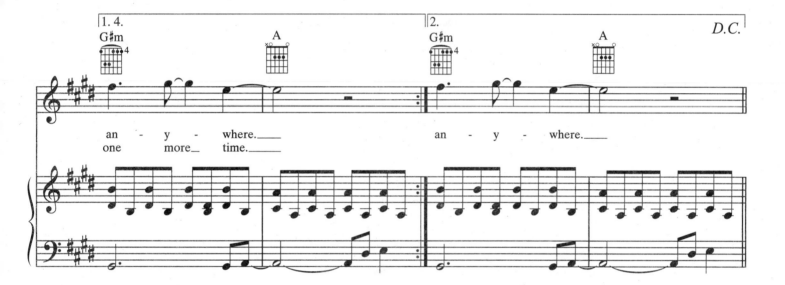

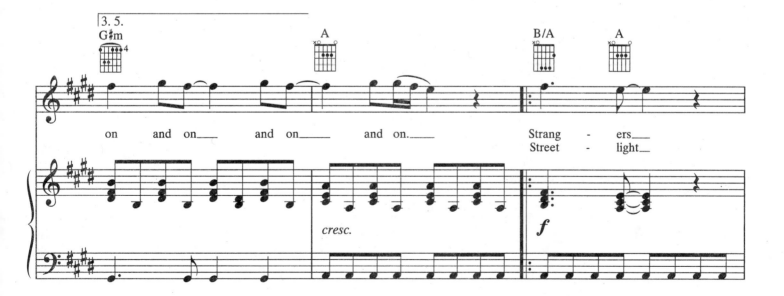

WHEEL IN THE SKY

Words and Music by
NEAL SCHON, ROBERT FLEISCHMAN
and DIANE VALORY

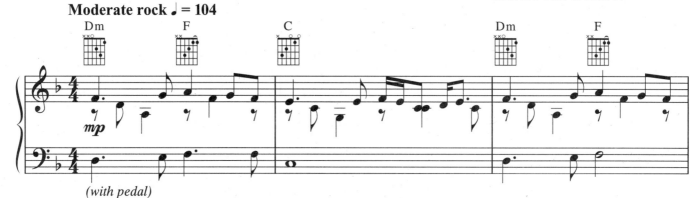

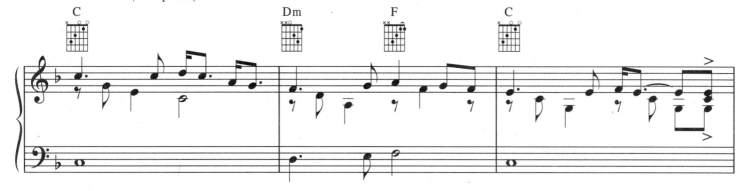

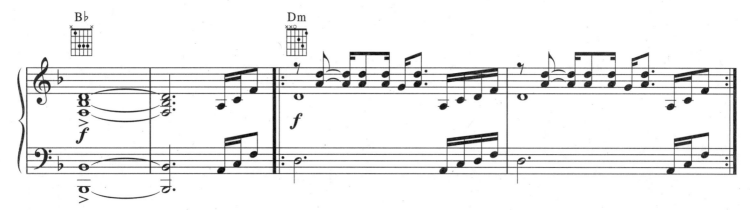

Verse:

1. Win-ter is here_ a - gain,_ oh Lord. Have-n't been home_ in a
2. I been try-in' to make it home._ Got to make it be -

8vb throughout

for to - mor - row.

Guitar solo ad lib.:

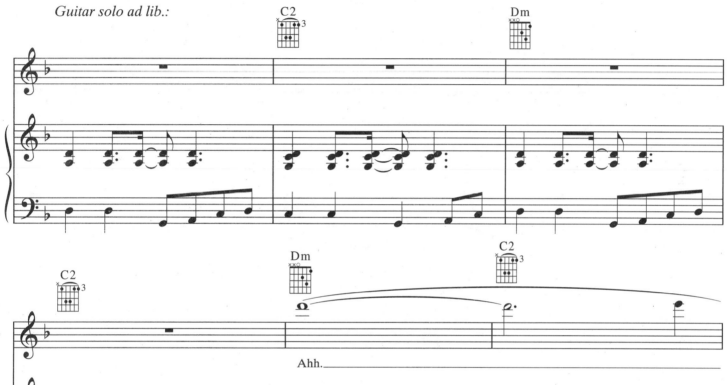

Ahh.

FAITHFULLY

Words and Music by
JONATHAN CAIN

faith - ful - ly._____

2. Cir - cus

Oh,_____ oh,_____

oh.

I'LL BE ALRIGHT WITHOUT YOU

Words and Music by
JONATHAN CAIN, NEAL SCHON
and STEVE PERRY

Verse 1:

1. I've been think-ing 'bout the times you walked_ out_ on me.

There were mo-ments I'd be-lieve you were_

26

WHO'S CRYING NOW

Words and Music by
JONATHAN CAIN and STEVE PERRY

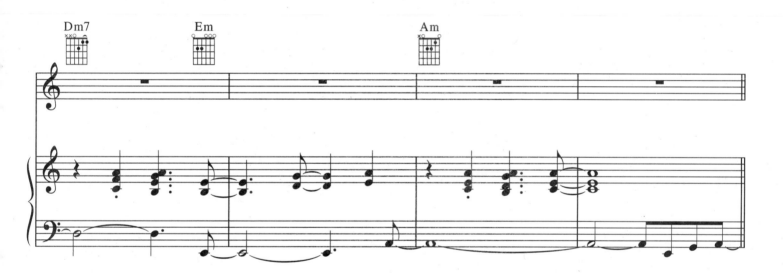

Who's Crying Now - 5 - 1
34646

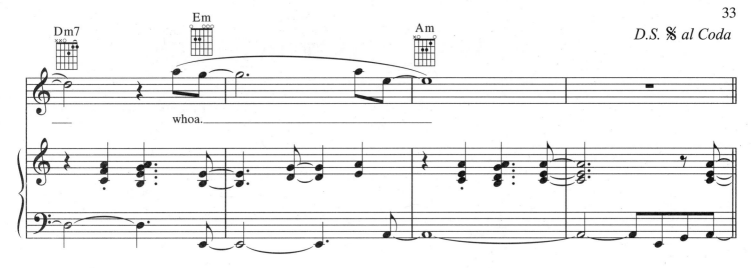

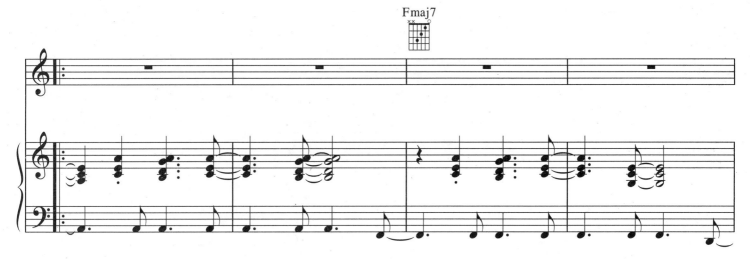

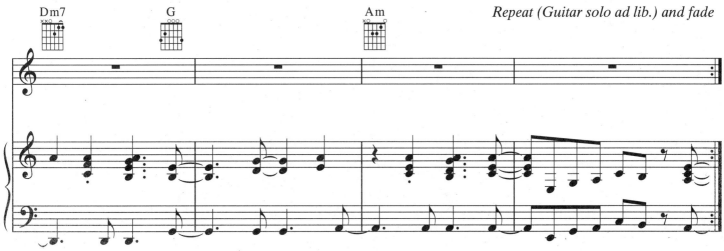

ANY WAY YOU WANT IT

Words and Music by
NEAL SCHON and STEVE PERRY

Moderately fast ♩ = 138

Verse:

Chorus:

ASK THE LONELY

Words and Music by
JONATHAN CAIN and STEVE PERRY

Moderately ♩ = 124

Verse:

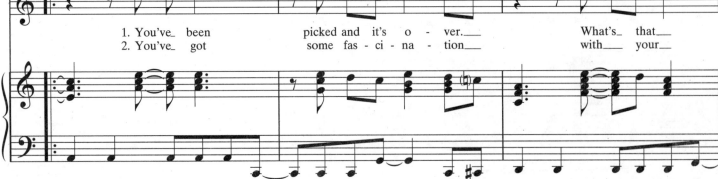

1. You've been picked and it's o - ver.___ What's that___
2. You've got some fas - ci - na - tion___ with___ your___

44

When you're feel-ing love's___ un-fair___ you just ask the lone - ly.

Chorus:

Repeat ad lib. and fade

SEPARATE WAYS
(Worlds Apart)

Words and Music by
JONATHAN CAIN and STEVE PERRY

Moderate fast rock ♩ = 132

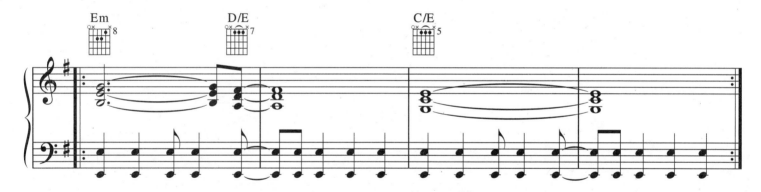

Verses 1 & 2:

1. Here we stand,___ world's a - part,___ hearts bro - ken in
2. Trou - bled times;___ caught be - tween___ con - fu - sion and

And if__ he ev - er hurts_ you, true_ love won't_ de - sert_ you.

No!_____

No!_____

LIGHTS

Words and Music by
NEAL SCHON and STEVE PERRY

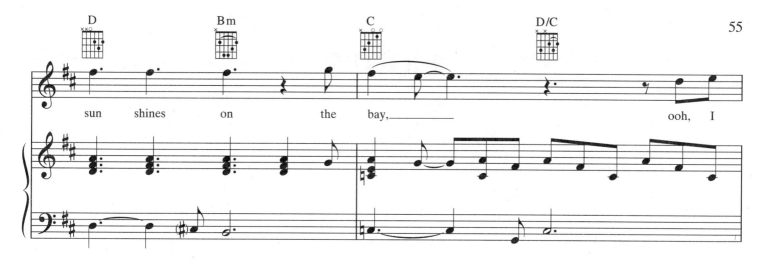

sun shines on the bay,_____ ooh, I

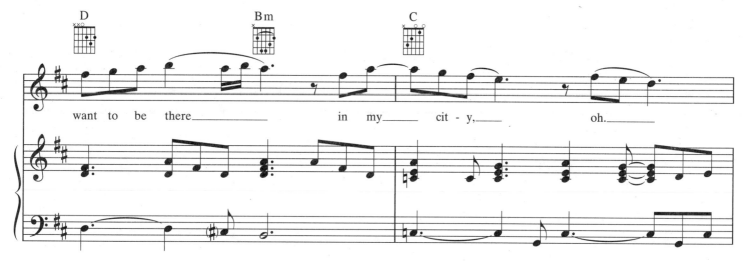

want to be there_____ in my____ cit - y,____ oh.____

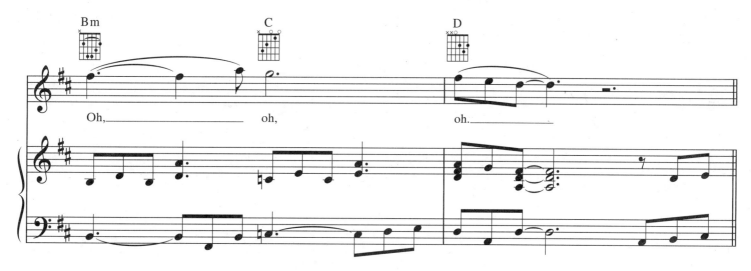

Oh,_____ oh, oh.____

Verse:

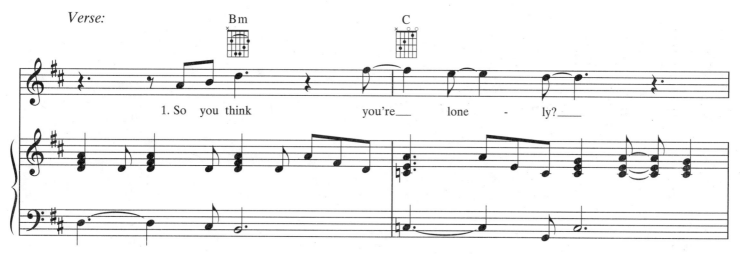

1. So you think you're___ lone - ly?____

Well, my friend,___ I'm lone-ly too.___

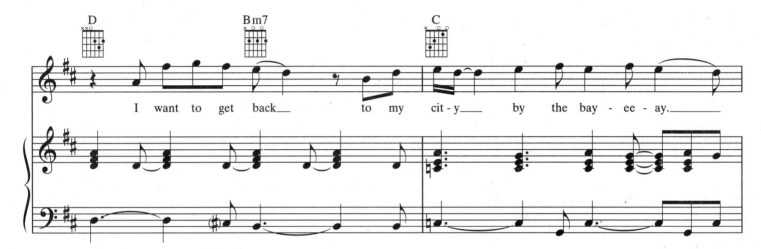

I want to get back___ to my cit-y___ by the bay - ee - ay.___

Oh, oh, oh.___ It's

Bridge:

sad,___ oh,___ there's been morn-ings out on the road with -
(2nd time - Guitar solo ad lib....

𝆑

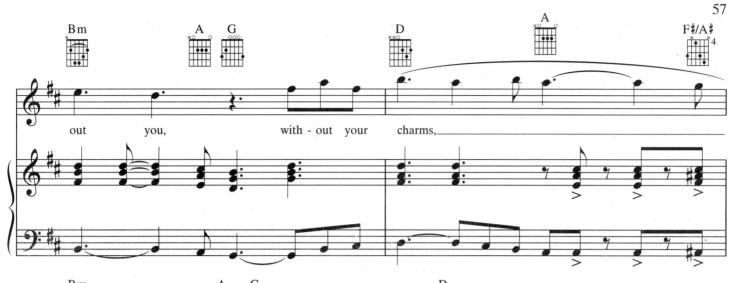

out you, with - out your charms,_____

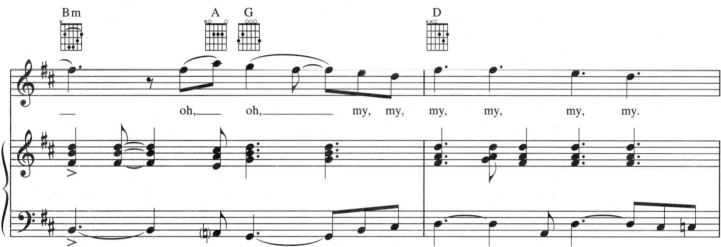

____ oh,___ oh,_____ my, my, my, my, my, my.

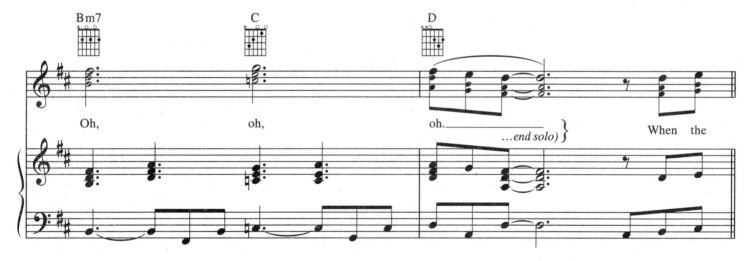

Oh, oh, oh._____ (...end solo) When the

Chorus:

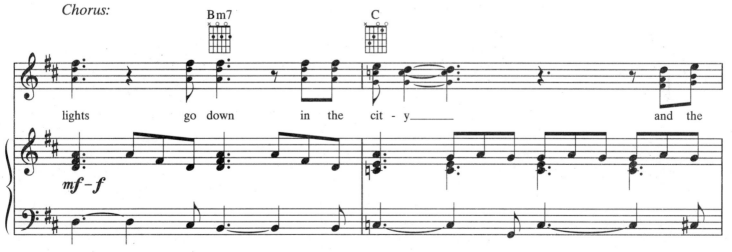

lights go down in the cit - y_____ and the

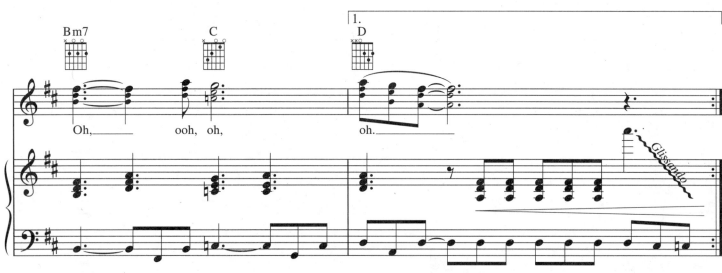

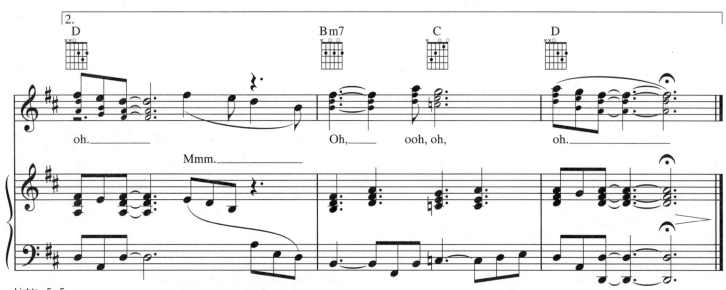

SEND HER MY LOVE

Words and Music by
JONATHAN CAIN and STEVE PERRY

Moderately, expressively ♩ = 126

Bridge:

LOVIN', TOUCHIN', SQUEEZIN'

Words and Music by
NEAL SCHON and STEVE PERRY

Verse 2 (sing 1st time only):

Verse 3 (sing 2nd time only):

oth - er. 2. When I'm a -

lone,_____ all___ by my - self,___

3. It won't be long, yes,___ till you're a - lone_____ when your

you're out lov - er, with some-one else.___ oh, he has - n't come home._ 'Cause he's

Chorus 1 (sing 1st time only):

Chorus 2 (sing 2nd time only):

68

Outro:

OPEN ARMS

Words and Music by
JONATHAN CAIN and STEVE PERRY

Chorus:

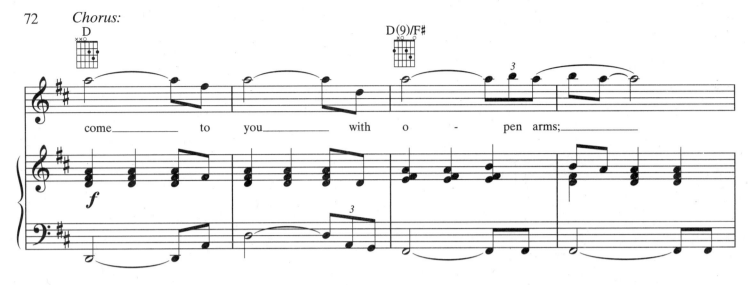

come_____ to you_____ with o - pen arms;_____

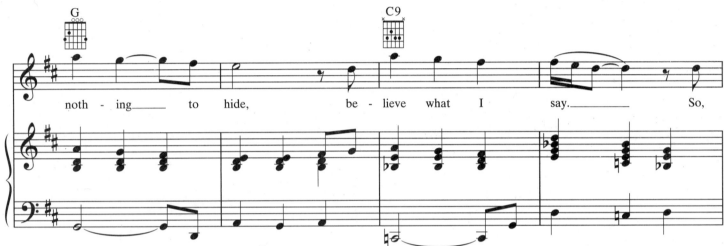

noth - ing_____ to hide, be - lieve what I say._____ So,

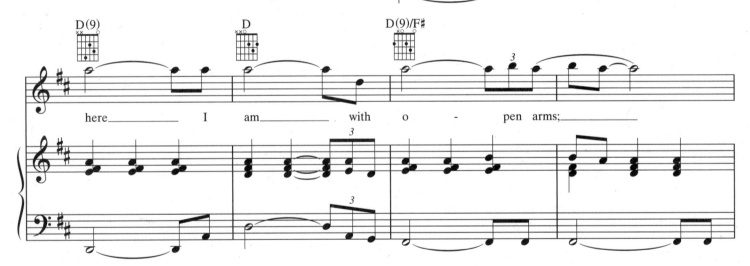

here_____ I am_____ with o - pen arms;_____

hop - ing you see what your love means___ to me,_____ o - pen

GIRL CAN'T HELP IT

Words and Music by
JONATHAN CAIN, NEAL SCHON
and STEVE PERRY

Moderately ♩ = 126

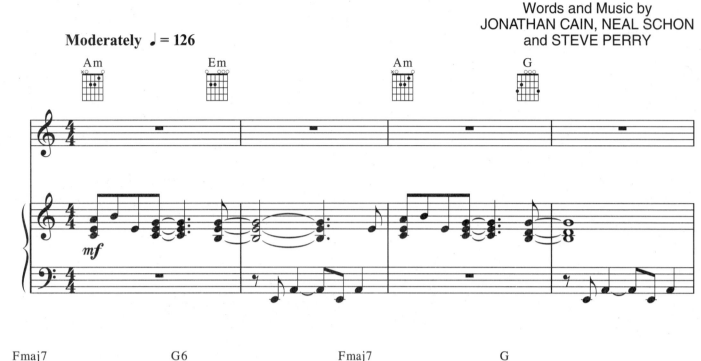

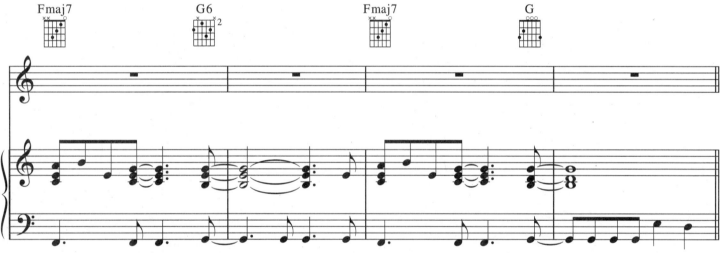

Verse:

1. If he could hold her so close in his
2. And when he calls her, she tells him that

(Oo,_____ there's a fire in his eyes for you._____

Oo,_____ don't you know she still cries for you._____)

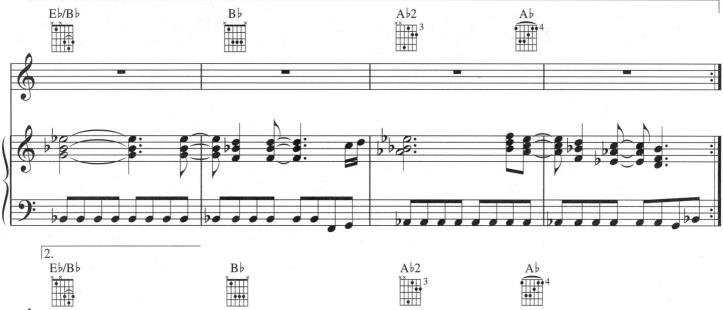

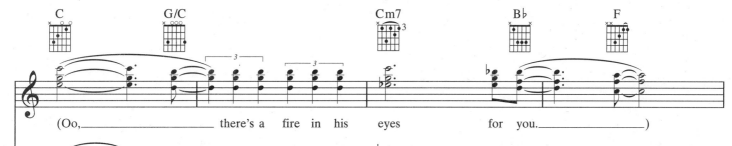

(Oo,_____ there's a fire in his eyes for you._____)

Oo,_____ noth-ing stands be-tween love and you._____)

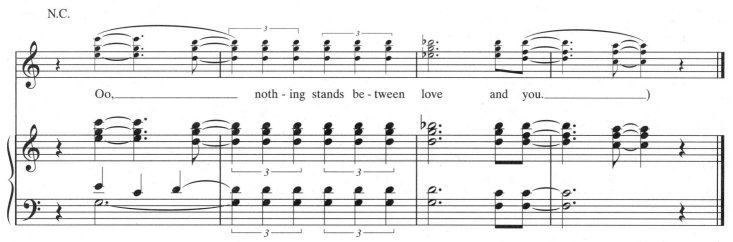

BE GOOD TO YOURSELF

Words and Music by
JONATHAN CAIN, NEAL SCHON
and STEVE PERRY

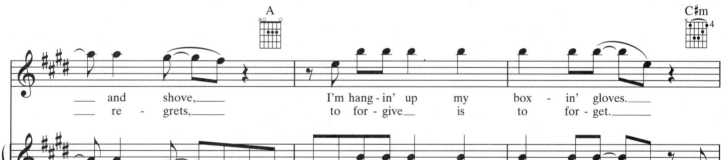

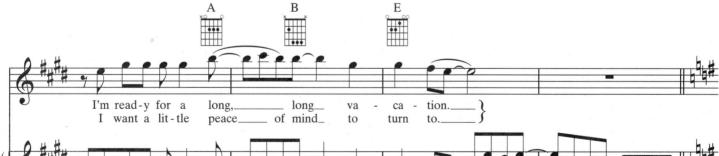

oh,_____ be good___ to your - self._____

___ to your - self._____

Chorus:

Be__ good._____ Be good___ to your - self when__

no - bod - y   else   will._____

Good._____

Guitar solo ad lib., repeat ad lib. and fade